NATIONAL GEOGRAPHIC

Ladders

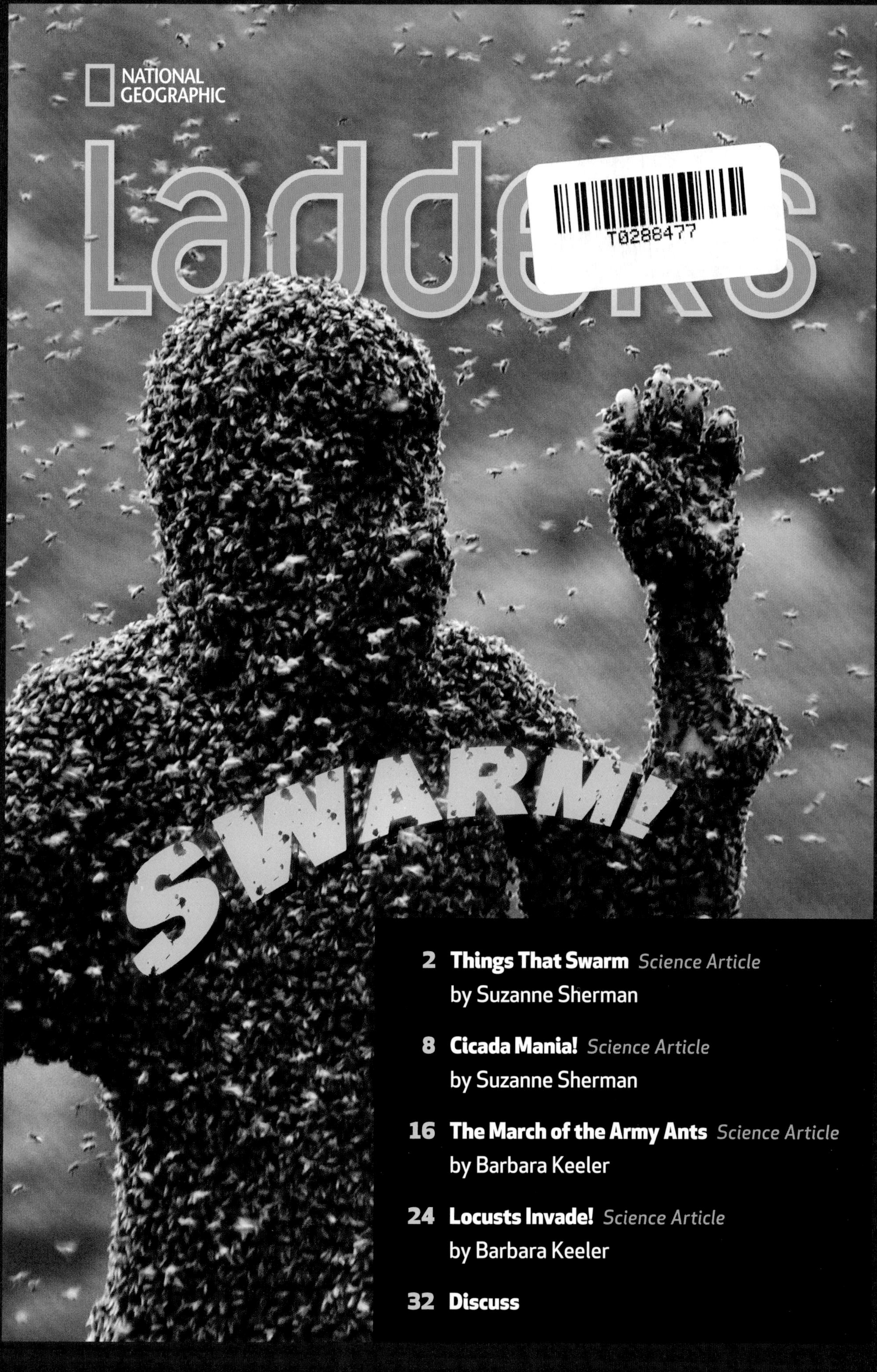

SWARM!

GENRE Science Article

Read to find out why some animals swarm for survival.

THINGS THAT SWAR

Every summer in Texas, millions of Mexican free-tailed bats huddle together in pitch darkness. They are females, caring for their pups in the safety of a large cave in the Eckert James River Bat Cave Preserve. They sleep hanging upside down by their feet during the day, emerging only at dusk. Then, as the sun begins to set, duck! A steady stream of hungry bats billows out of the cave, darkening the sky.

Don't worry, the bats aren't interested in you—they are on the hunt for food. The bats dip, dive, and swirl through the sky, catching insects like moths and mosquitoes. Incredibly, they don't bump into each other even as they reach speeds approaching 97 kilometers (about 60 miles) per hour! As more bats join in, the group begins to circle like a tornado, forming a dark cloud so vast that it may be seen from a mile away.

by Suzanne Sherman

How do bats maneuver around each other so well? For one thing, bats have flexible wings that allow them to weave and turn quickly in flight. They also have a special system of locating objects, called echolocation. To use echolocation, bats send out a series of high-pitched chirping sounds. When the sounds reach an object, they echo, or bounce back. The bats' brains use the echoes to "see" in the dark.

When bats or another large group of animals comes together, scientists call it a **swarm.** Bats are not the only animals that fly in a swarm—the insects the bats are chasing fly in a swarm, too. A flock of birds settling on a tree branch is a swarm, and so is a school of fish darting through the water. Whatever we call it, a large gathering of animals can be quite an amazing sight.

RED CRABS

A swarm of adult red crabs migrates to the shore for breeding. The males arrive first, followed by the females who soon outnumber them.

A rippling, crawling, red carpet seems to cover lawns, schoolyards, and parks. With a clacking of claws and legs, swarms of red crabs scrabble across the roads. Over fifty million crabs are on the move on Christmas Island, a territory of Australia.

During the wet season in October, November, and December, swarms of red crabs **migrate** from the forested areas of the island to the ocean shore where they breed. When animals migrate, they travel from one region to another as the seasons change. The crabs stream down tall cliffs and brave human-made obstacles, including roads. Year after year, they follow the same route.

At the ocean, males dig burrows on the shore. After mating, the males make their way back to the forests. Females

stay in the burrow for a time, and then release their eggs into the ocean. The eggs hatch into tiny **larvae** upon contact with the water. The larvae grow through several stages, finally becoming young crabs. Then they return to shore and journey back to the forest.

PENGUINS

Whipped by gale force winds and blizzards, Emperor penguins march single file for miles. Like many animals, they form huge swarms when they are ready to reproduce.

Every year, Emperor penguins leave the sea and make their way to their inland breeding grounds in Antarctica. Their destination is so cold and barren that predators are scarce. There, the penguins pair up to mate. Each female lays a single egg and then treks back to the ocean with the other females to feed. The males remain, huddled in a huge group for warmth, to protect and incubate the eggs. During this time they have nothing to eat.

After about two months, the eggs hatch. The females return to feed and care for the chicks while the starved, ravenous males return to the ocean to feed. When the chicks are old enough to swim and feed, all the penguins return to the sea, where they are most exposed to the elements.

Adult penguins swarm around their chicks to protect them against the cold. The penguins take turns being on the outside.

Dense flocks of starlings form complex patterns as they evade predators.

STARLINGS

The saying "safety in numbers" seems to apply to starlings. Flocks of between 10,000 and a million starlings form gigantic clouds that darken the sky and change shape like black smoke. These huge flocks of starlings swarm together as they fly to feed on grains from farm fields.

Forming a swarm provides protection for the birds and helps them find food, as a large flock has more eyes to spot food and predators. A starling that sees a predator veers away from it, causing the birds closest to it react and veer in the same direction, and the birds closest to them do likewise. This coordinated behavior results in a complex pattern of movement for the whole flock. An entire flock of birds can make even hairpin turns very quickly.

A tree branch provides a suitable resting spot for a swarm of honeybees. The queen gives off a chemical that the others can smell. That keeps the group together as scout bees search for a new place to nest.

If you have ever seen a swarm of honeybees, it might have seemed scary. A swarm may include between 1,500 and 30,000 bees, all flying close together. Honeybees are not dangerous when they swarm, however. They usually sting only around their nests, where they need to protect their young and their food supply. When they are swarming, they have no young or food to protect.

HONEYBEES

Swarming is instinctive behavior; the bees do not have to learn how to do it. When a nest gets crowded, thousands of workers, some drones, and a queen fly off together to start a new colony. They settle on a tree limb or bush and wait while scout bees look for a place to nest. After the scouts find a suitable cavity, such as a hollow tree, the bees move in. The workers begin building combs and the queen begins laying eggs.

Whether to find food, to breed, for protection, or to find a new home, many animals form vast swarms. For these animals, survival means sticking together.

Check In How does swarming help animals survive? Think of some specific examples.

GENRE Science Article

Read to find out about the amazing lives of cicadas.

Cicada Mania!

by Suzanne Sherman

Imagine a million black, shrimp-size insects with huge wings and beady red eyes staring at you! These insects only come out in the summer, hiding underground the rest of the year. When they emerge, they often do so in great numbers, filling the air with a loud buzzing sound that many people think sounds like summer itself. They are cicadas. They quickly crawl up trees and suck their liquids, living on the food the trees have made using the sun's energy.

There are more than 3,000 cicada species that emerge from the earth. Certain species of cicadas are called annual because some individuals emerge every year. They live about two years or more and the adults emerge over an entire summer. Some annual cicadas are very dark with greenish markings. As frightening as cicadas can look, they are harmless to humans.

Some cicadas, known as periodical cicadas, can be identified by their bright red eyes. They live only in the United States east of the Great Plains. Periodical cicadas live long lives underground and come up from the ground all at once, every 13 or 17 years, forming huge **swarms.** Up to 40,000 cicadas can emerge from under a single tree, quickly climbing trees and poles.

After they emerge, their only purpose is to mate. The male dies shortly after mating and the female lives just long enough to lay eggs. Even after they're gone, empty cicada shells, or exoskeletons, still hang from trees. Piles of exoskeletons cover the bases of trees and even sidewalks.

Notice the beady red eyes and lacy wings of these periodical cicadas.

Growing Up Underground

A cicada lives most of its life hidden beneath the ground we walk on. As it grows, it goes through **incomplete metamorphosis.** It hatches as a nymph that looks like its parents, but smaller. The nymph **molts,** or sheds its exoskeleton, several times as its body grows.

The adult cicada leaves its exoskeleton still clinging to the tree as it flies away.

On the surface, the nymph molts for the last time, emerging as an adult. Its soft, pale body will harden and darken within an hour.

In the spring of its 13th or 17th year, the nymph constructs an exit tunnel to the surface. You can see these as small holes in the ground.

After mating, females lay their eggs in twigs. A female cicada has a pointed abdomen with a needle-shaped structure called an ovipositor. The female uses the ovipositor to slice into wood and deposit rows of eggs.

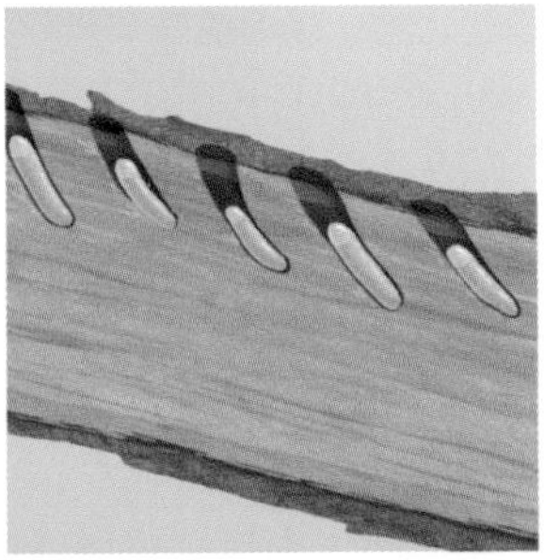

Between one and several dozen eggs can be laid in one slit in one branch. Each female can lay as many as 400 eggs total. The eggs hatch after six to ten weeks.

After hatching, the small, ant-sized **nymph** falls to the ground where it will burrow into the soil.

Underground, the nymph feeds on liquids from plant roots. The roots contain energy the tree has converted from sunlight. The nymph grows steadily, molting several times.

What's the Buzz?

Shrill buzzing and clicking sounds fill the air, sometimes almost as loud as a jet airplane! All male cicadas are famous for their loud, droning mating call. Some calls can be heard from half a mile away.

This racket is essential to cicada survival. Before females can lay eggs, they need to find mates. The silent females locate mates by the males' songs. Each species has its own song, and different species sing at different times of the day. Some sing in the early part of the day, others at midday, and others sing in the late afternoon.

The males are not hard to find; the song of just one periodical cicada can be as loud as nearly 90 decibels. If you were standing next to one single male, its song may sound as loud as a power lawn mower! Males do not sing alone, however; they gather to sing in choruses that are even louder.

Cicada songs sound so much like machines that cicadas are attracted to power tools such as lawnmowers, weed cutters, and hedge trimmers. Females mistake these machines for males singing. Males mistake the machine noises for a chorus of other males and rush to join in.

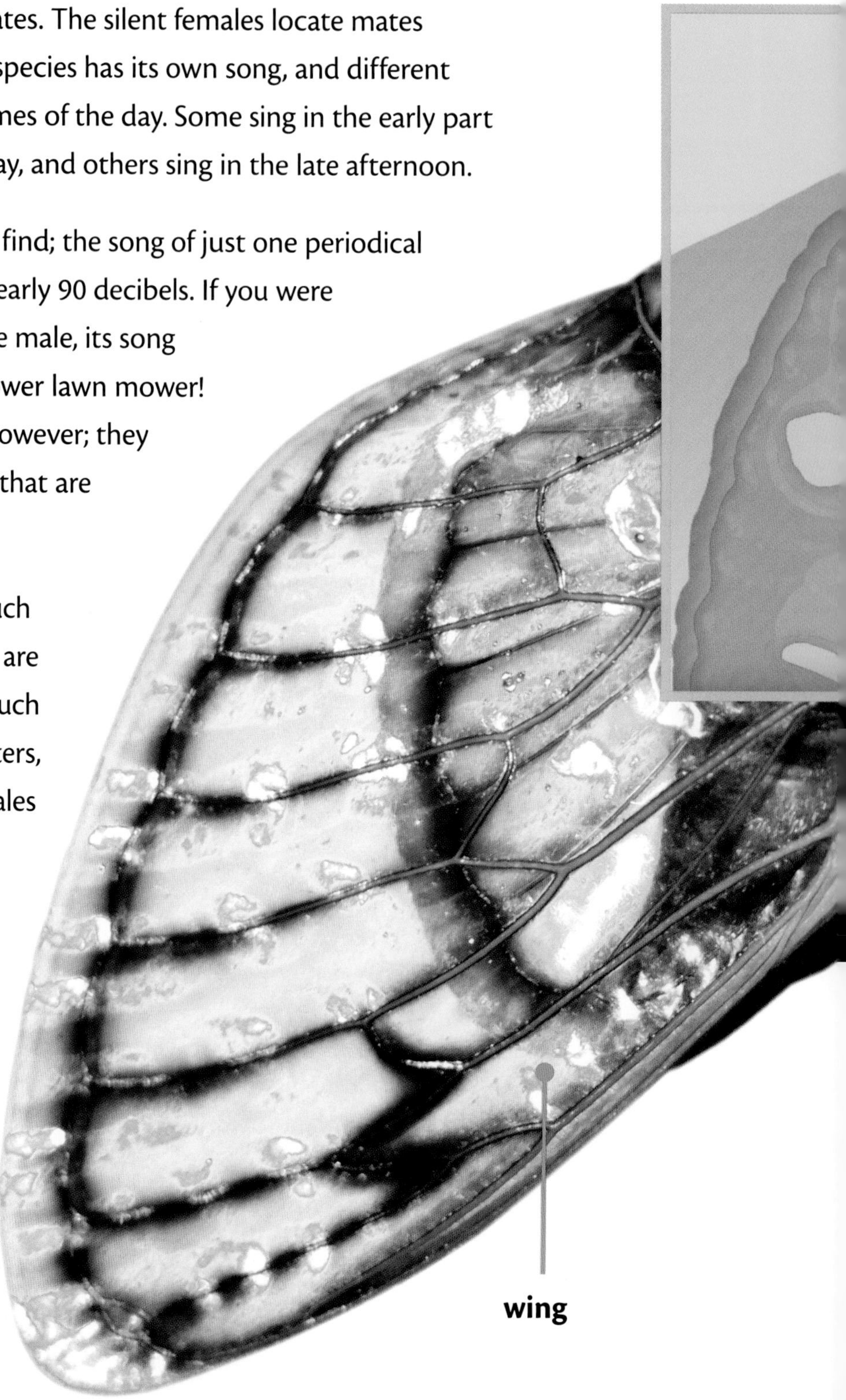

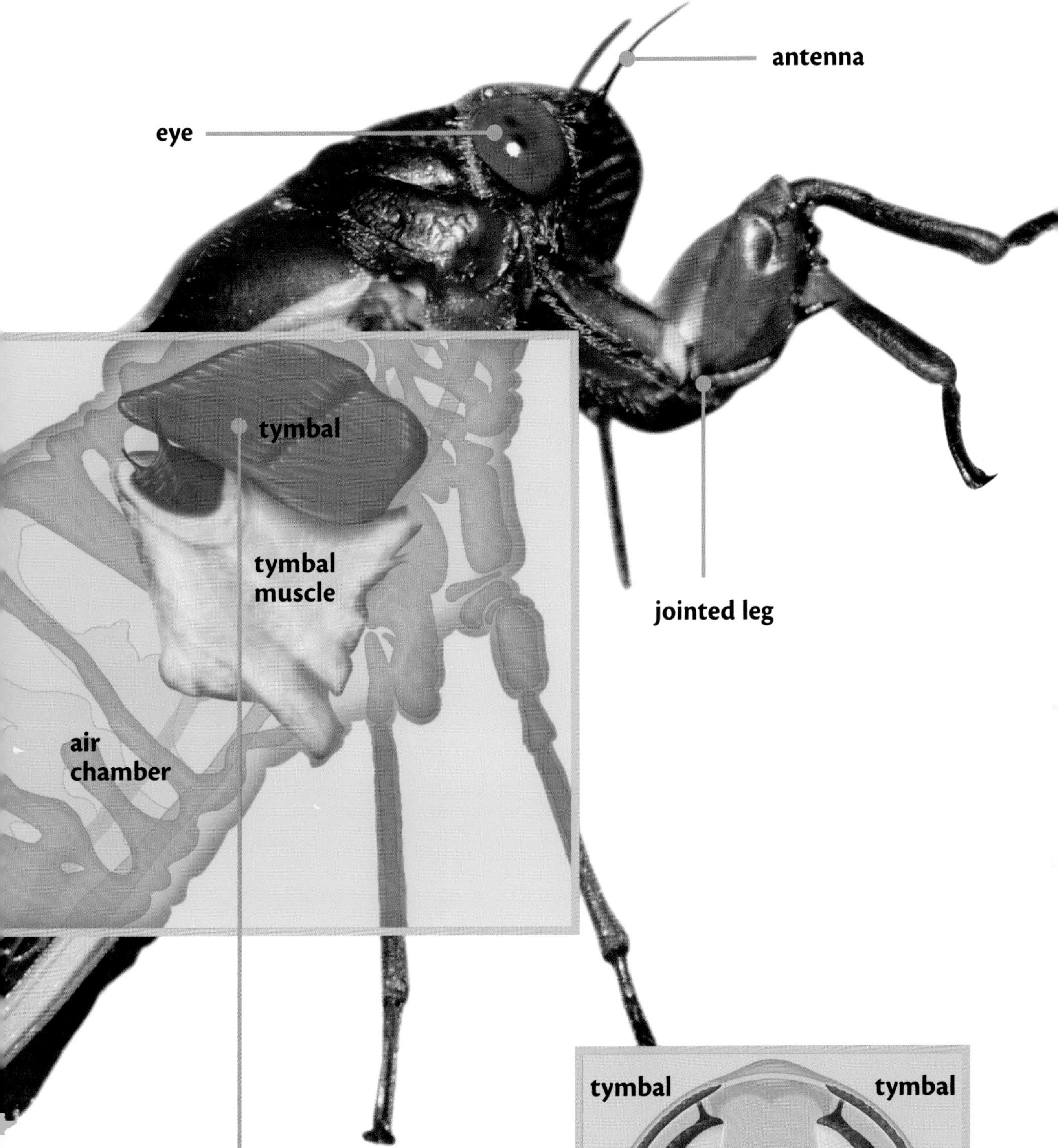

Male cicadas have a membrane on each side of their bodies called a tymbal. Internal muscles move the tymbals back and forth rapidly, which produces a fast series of clicking noises that we hear as a buzzing sound.

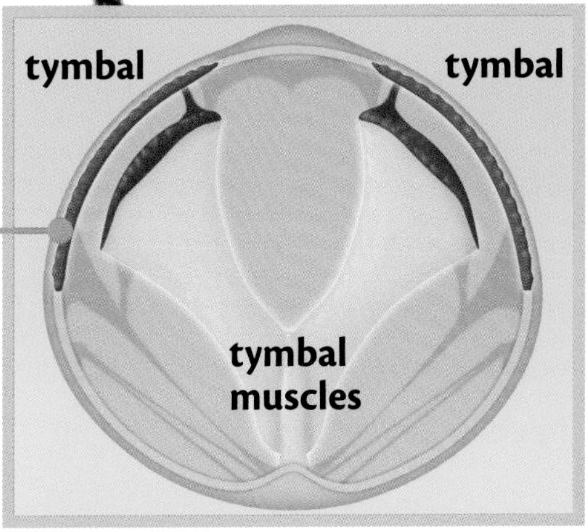

This image shows another view of the inside of the male's body. You can see the two tymbal membranes and the muscles that move them.

Too Much to Eat

Cicadas are a predator's perfect prey—they don't fight, they are highly nutritious, and they taste great! They are also low in fat and high in protein. Many kinds of animals gorge on cicadas—birds, squirrels, dogs, cats, turtles, fish, and spiders, for example. Even people eat them. On the Internet, you can find recipes for roasted cicadas, cicada pizza, cicada tacos, cicada dumplings, cicada cookies, and cicada pie. Most recipes will tell you to collect them when the cicadas emerge from the final molting, before the exoskeleton of the adult has hardened.

Periodical cicadas use an unusual survival strategy: stuff the predators! Cicadas emerge in such huge numbers that their predators fill up and stop eating. The predators cannot possibly eat all of the cicadas, so billions of cicadas survive to reproduce. This strategy does not work so well for the cicadas that are eaten, but it works splendidly for the individuals that are left over.

Most of all, the strategy works for future generations and the survival of the species. By emerging in huge swarms for protection, periodical cicadas enable most of their members to survive.

A rainbow bee-eater feasts on a cicada in Northern Territory, Australia. Many different species of cicadas can be found all over the world.

Check In Why do cicadas swarm?

GENRE Science Article

Read to find out how army ants swarm to hunt, reproduce, and protect themselves.

THE MARCH OF THE

by Barbara Keeler

An estimated ten thousand trillion ants crawl in and on the earth. Their combined weight is about the same as the combined weight of all humans! In almost every ecosystem—grasslands, forests, deserts, and wetlands—ants work thanklessly cleaning up small dead invertebrates and preying on living ones. So far, scientists have identified 12,000 species of ants.

One species of army ant, *Eciton burchellii,* lives in Central and South America. These ants live in huge colonies of about 300,000 or more individual ants, and their approach to hunting food is ferocious—army ants hunt as a **swarm.**

Army ants are among the world's most ferocious hunters. Their powerful scissor-like jaws, called mandibles, are not used for eating, but for tearing, crushing, and biting. Army ants can only swallow liquefied food.

Although they are blind, a swarm of army ants can easily overcome prey. With their blade-like jaws, they can hack and dice much larger prey, such as scorpions and tarantulas. Non-prey animals, such as lizards, snakes, and frogs, are killed if they are in the way.

Different kinds of workers have different mandibles. Guard ants use giant mandibles to protect the smaller workers. Soldier ants have medium-sized mandibles that they use to capture prey and cut it into pieces the ants can carry.

ARMY ANTS

Eciton burchellii can be found in many countries from Mexico to central South America.

ON THE HUNT

Hundreds of thousands of army ants leave the nest in search of prey. They fan out in a dense swarm as wide as 14 meters (about 15 yards). That would be like the entire population of a city going on a hunt together!

THE LIFE OF AN ARMY ANT

Unlike most ants, army ants do not live in permanent homes. When they are not hunting, they stay in one place for about three weeks. During this time, the queen lays eggs. When the eggs hatch, newly hatched **larvae** need to be fed, so the ants go on the move and the hunting begins again. When the larvae develop into **pupae,** the ants again stay in one place. The queen lays some more eggs. When the pupae develop into adults, the colony goes on the move again.

When the colony is not on the move, army ants form temporary above-ground nests. They use unusual building materials: their own bodies! In a partly sheltered location, workers link their legs and bodies together with strong hooked claws at the tips of their feet. They form a solid cylindrical or spherical mass, about a meter in diameter. The nest even has tunnels and walls.

The large ant, a queen, may lay more than 100,000 eggs. Workers take care of the queen.

An egg hatches as a white larva. The larva stage lasts about 15 days.

Adults can be queens, male drones, or workers. A worker is shown in the photo. Only the queens and drones reproduce.

During the pupa stage, the larva changes to an adult. Other ants carry the pupae.

Inside the nest, the larvae and pupae do not look anything like adult ants. This is because ants undergo **complete metamorphosis,** meaning they are born looking very different from the adults. Ants have four life stages. From the egg, an ant hatches as a grub-like larva. The larva later becomes a pupa. In the pupa stage, the insect's body form changes until an adult emerges. The adult is either a queen, male drone, or worker. Each has a different role in the colony.

AN UNUSUAL NURSERY

The colony's queen and thousands of eggs, larvae, and pupae are safe near the center of this unusual nest.

WORK TO DO

In your school, all workers probably do not do the same job. Different workers teach the classes, clean the rooms, weed the garden, serve the food, and run the office. Different kinds of ants also perform specialized tasks for the colony. A male drone's only job is to mate with the queen, and the queen's job is to lay eggs. The army ant species *Eciton burchellii* also has different types of workers: majors, submajors, and minors.

A LIVING BRIDGE

When army ants come across a gap in their path, it doesn't stop them. Workers link their bodies together to form a bridge.

A colony has a single queen whose only job is to lay eggs. Its body expands and turns white during reproduction.

A drone is a male with wings; its only job is to mate. In this photograph, two workers are hitching a ride on a drone.

Majors, or guard ants, are the largest of the worker ants. With their giant mandibles, guard army ants protect the other ants from predators.

Submajors, or soldiers, are a little smaller than the guard ants. Their main job is to hunt, capture prey, and carry it to the colony.

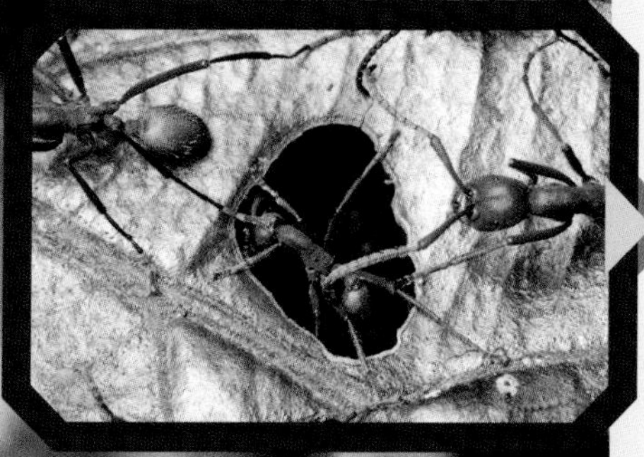

Worker minors are the smallest army ants and they help carry food. They sometimes lie down and use their bodies to even out a path for other workers.

PEST CONTROL

At first it might seem that these fierce, swarming army ants are destructive to ecosystems. They are, however, an important part of the food chain. As consumers, they eat many animals, including tarantulas, scorpions, other ants, wasps, beetles, roaches, and grasshoppers. Some of these insects are agricultural pests, and army ants help control their populations. Army ants also clean up by eating small dead bodies. The ants themselves become meals for many birds and mammals, which are usually not threatened by army ants.

For many other predators, an army ant swarm is like a full dinner table. Small animals in the path of an army ant swarm panic, try to escape, and are not on the alert for other predators. It is easy for predators to spot small animals hopping,

AMAZING ARMY ANTS

- More than 200 species of army ants live on Earth.
- A single army ant can carry about 20 times its weight.
- An army ant queen only needs to mate once. From that one mating, it may lay as many as 120,000 eggs over a lifetime.
- In East Africa, driver army ants have been used to keep wounds closed. The ants lock their huge mandibles on the wound and do not let go.
- Army ants create their own garbage dumps. There they pile all the hard bits of prey, such as insect legs, that they cannot eat.
- Some animals have special escape mechanisms they use during army ant swarms. Stick insects take advantage of the army ant's blindness. They become motionless, so the ants do not detect them and attack.

flying, and scrambling out of the swarm's path. In fact, animals such as monkeys and birds sometimes follow a migrating army ant colony so they can catch insects, spiders, and small animals as they flee.

All ants swarm to find food, to reproduce, and for protection. Army ants also hunt and kill in one huge, vicious swarm. A swarm of army ants is almost like one gigantic predator!

LITTLE ANTS—BIG JOB

Army ants play an important role as ecosystem predators. This cricket is an easy prey for a swarm of army ants.

Check In What are some ways army ants benefit the ecosystem?

GENRE **Science Article**

Read to find out how desert locusts swarm to find food.

Locusts Invade!

by Barbara Keeler

Like a huge, dark cloud, a locust **swarm** sweeps through the sky, blocking out sunlight. Throughout history, swarms of locusts have struck terror in the hearts of humans, and for good reason. They can wipe out crops and bring famine to people who depend on the crops. Locust swarms still do horrendous damage to crops in some parts of the world today. Each locust can eat its weight in plants in one day. Together, a swarm of locusts can eat 192 million kilograms (423 million pounds) of plants every day, and locusts will devour just about any crop.

Found in Africa, the Middle East, and Asia, desert locusts live in 60 countries. Desert locusts in Africa cause major crop damage that can lead to human famine and starvation. Desert locusts today can affect the well-being of one-tenth of the world's humans.

Like other species of grasshoppers, desert locusts are sometimes solitary insects. Unlike other grasshoppers, however, locusts have another phase in which they form huge, hungry swarms. A desert locust swarm can include billions of insects: between 40 and 80 million insects per square kilometer, stretched over 1,191 square kilometers (460 square miles). These swarms can cover a vast territory as they **migrate** across entire countries.

The Desert Locust

Like all insects, locusts do not have lungs. Instead, insects have a series of openings on the sides of their bodies. Oxygen is taken in through the openings and carbon dioxide is given off.

A locust has a pair of membranes on the first segment of the abdomen near the base of the legs. These membranes detect vibrations from the environment, which enable the locust to "hear."

A pair of antennae help the locust recognize things by touch or smell.

A locust has compound eyes composed of many lenses. The locust has a wide field of vision to detect movement.

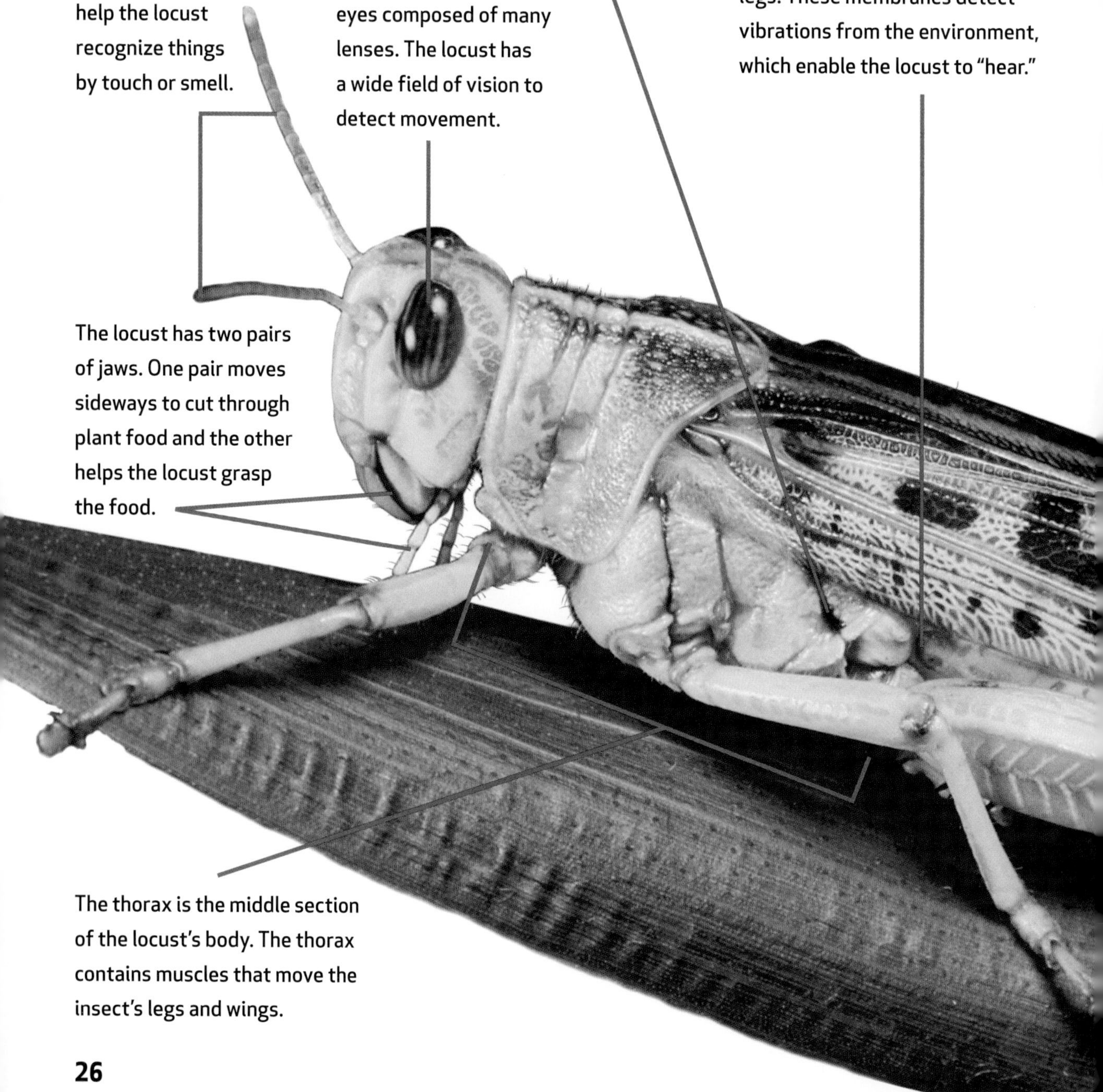

The locust has two pairs of jaws. One pair moves sideways to cut through plant food and the other helps the locust grasp the food.

The thorax is the middle section of the locust's body. The thorax contains muscles that move the insect's legs and wings.

The locust goes through three stages in its life cycle: egg, **nymph,** and adult. The life cycle of the locust is considered an **incomplete metamorphosis** because the nymphs, or hoppers, resemble the adults. Nymphs are smaller than the adults and cannot reproduce, but the other features of their bodies are similar.

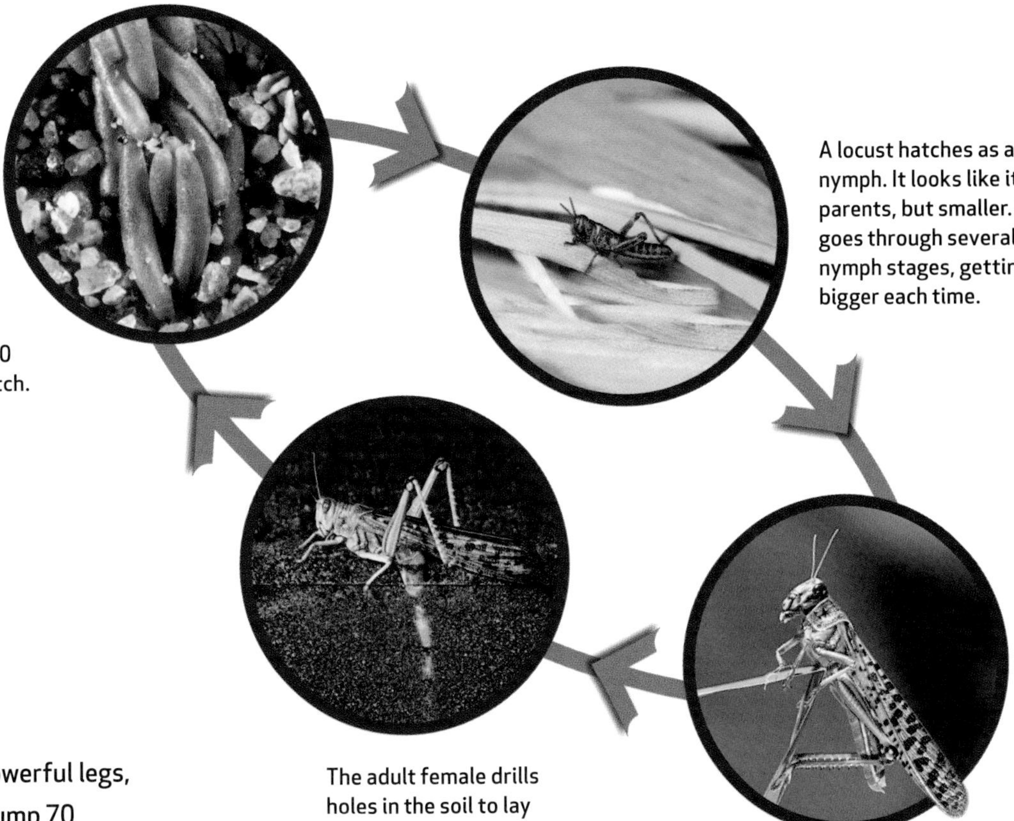

A locust begins life as an egg. There may be 30 to 50 eggs in one batch.

A locust hatches as a nymph. It looks like its parents, but smaller. It goes through several nymph stages, getting bigger each time.

The adult is solitary unless it is mating or swarming.

The adult female drills holes in the soil to lay batches of eggs.

With their powerful legs, locusts can jump 70 centimeters (2.3 feet).

Grouping Together

What causes a calm, solitary locust with a modest appetite to change into an aggressive, ravenous, swarming pest? The desert locust lives a solitary life as long as food is plentiful over a wide area. Locusts are consumers in the food chain; they consume plants. In turn, the plants are producers—they have used energy from the sun to make their own food.

When the land dries up and food is available in fewer areas, the search for food brings locusts closer together. As they crowd into the areas where plants still grow, the hind legs of the insects bump together. Sensitive hairs on the legs detect the touch and cause changes in the locust's body and behavior. Their color transforms to black and yellow or orange. Males become bright yellow.

A locust that is about to swarm has three times more of a chemical called serotonin than a solitary locust. Serotonin is a chemical in animals and humans that affects mood and behavior. The locusts become irritable and restless and develop enormous appetites. They give off chemical signals that cause them to band together and swarm.

Billions of ravenous locusts rage across the skies and chomp their way through the land. They devour crops and other vegetation, leaving large patches of cleared land behind them. They have even been said to raid people's homes and consume their food and clothing.

Swarms can also cover vast distances. A swarm traveled from northwest Africa to Great Britain in 1954. In 1988, another flew from West Africa to the Caribbean.

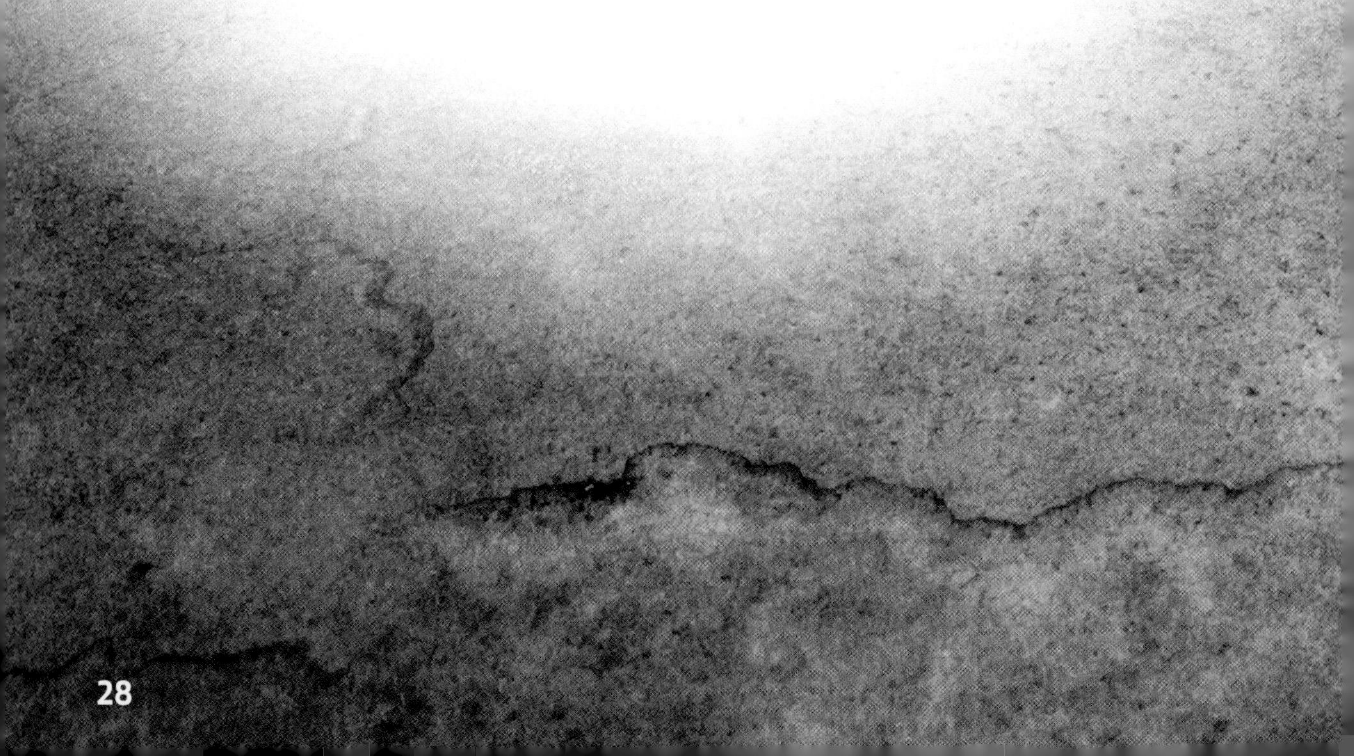

The green area on the map shows where desert locusts live when they are not swarming. The yellow area shows how far the swarms can spread.

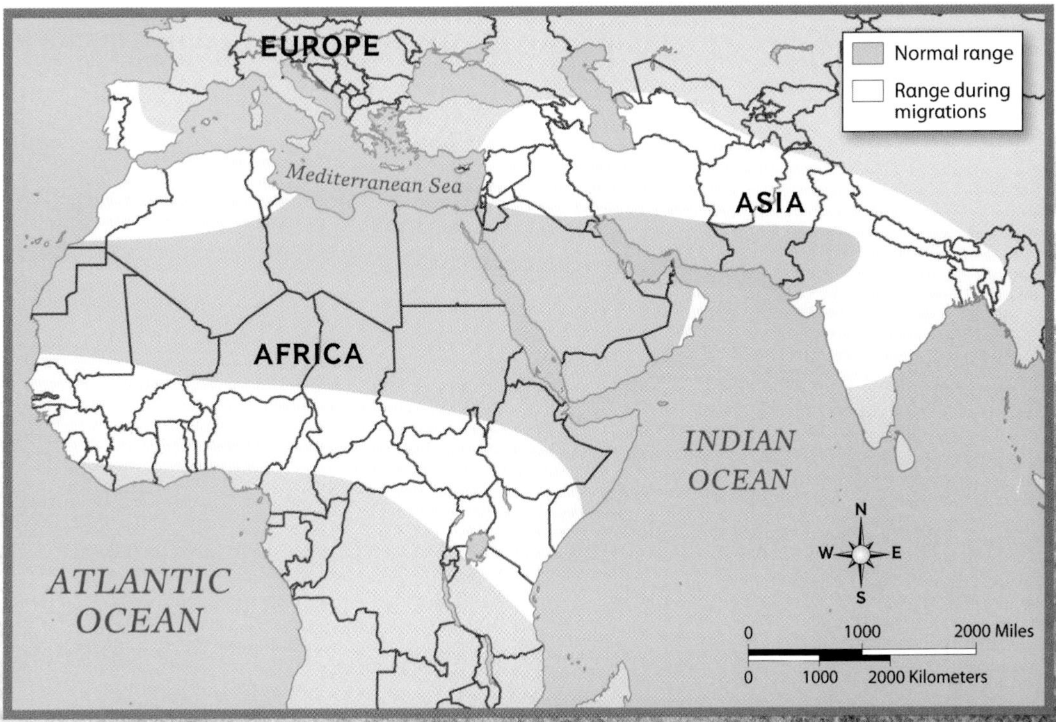

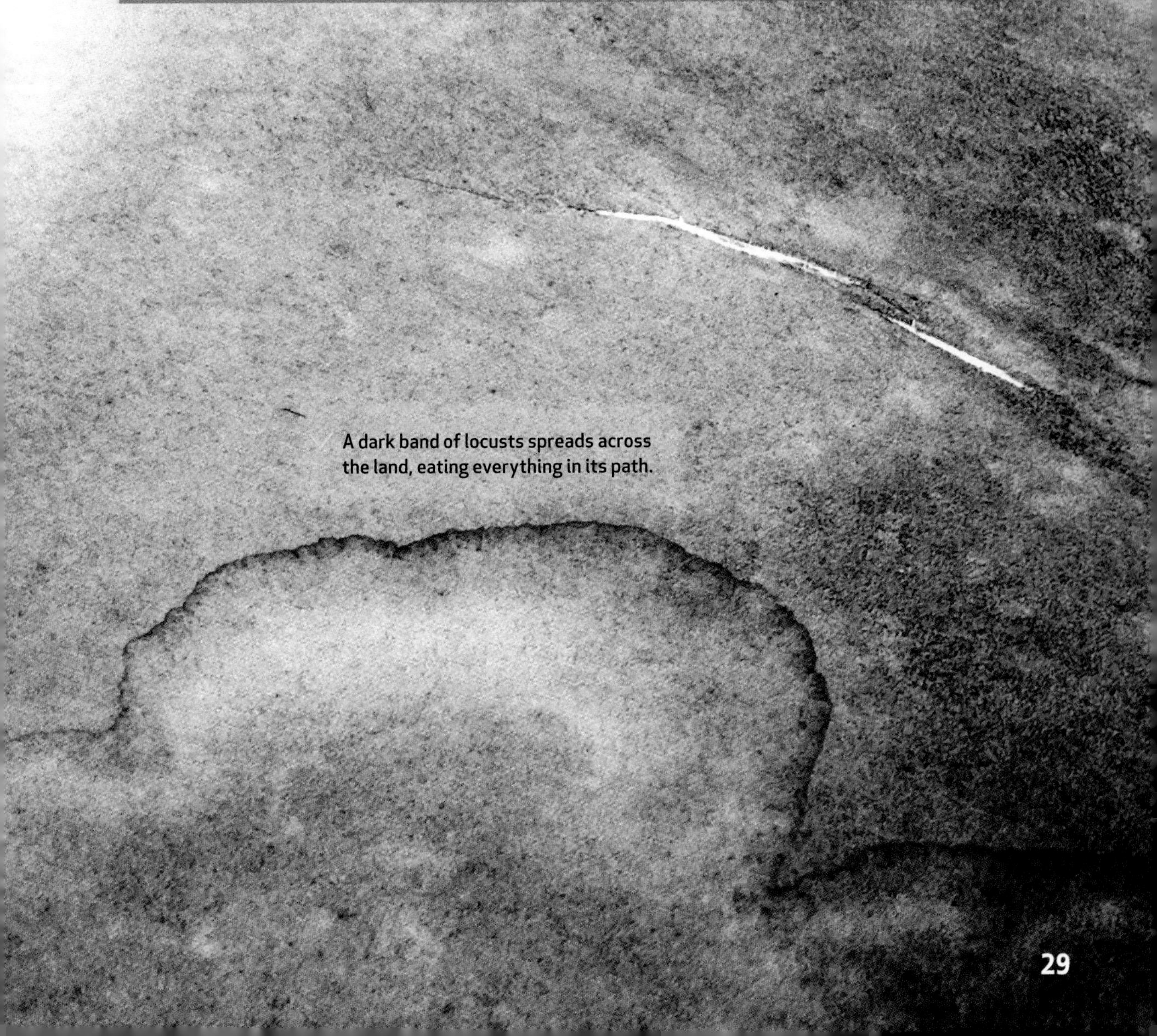

A dark band of locusts spreads across the land, eating everything in its path.

The Rocky Mountain Locust

The swarm loomed on the horizon like a menacing dark cloud. In 1875, trillions of locusts swept through the land like a living tornado 2,896 kilometers (1,799 miles) long. The swarm spread north towards North Dakota and west to the Rocky Mountains, leaving a wake of devastation and destruction.

One witness said, "The locusts came down from the sky like hail. Frightened people ran into their homes as the locusts' claws dug into their skin and hung upon their clothing."

Rocky Mountain locusts devastated parts of North America for hundreds of years, but now North America is locust free. The locusts simply vanished. At the University of Wyoming, scientist Jeff Lockwood investigated why the Rocky Mountain locust disappeared.

First, Lockwood looked for locust bodies trapped in glacial ice in the Rocky Mountains. For centuries, strong winds would sweep swarms of locusts high into the mountains. There they would freeze to death. From studying the bodies, Lockwood could tell that the Rocky Mountain locust didn't decline over a long period. "In fact, what we're looking at is a very sudden, sort of bolt out of the blue disappearance," said Lockwood.

Huge piles of Rocky Mountain locusts had to be shoveled off train tracks. Their crushed bodies made the tracks too slippery for the trains to run.

Scientist Jeff Lockwood searches for Rocky Mountain locust remains frozen in a glacier.

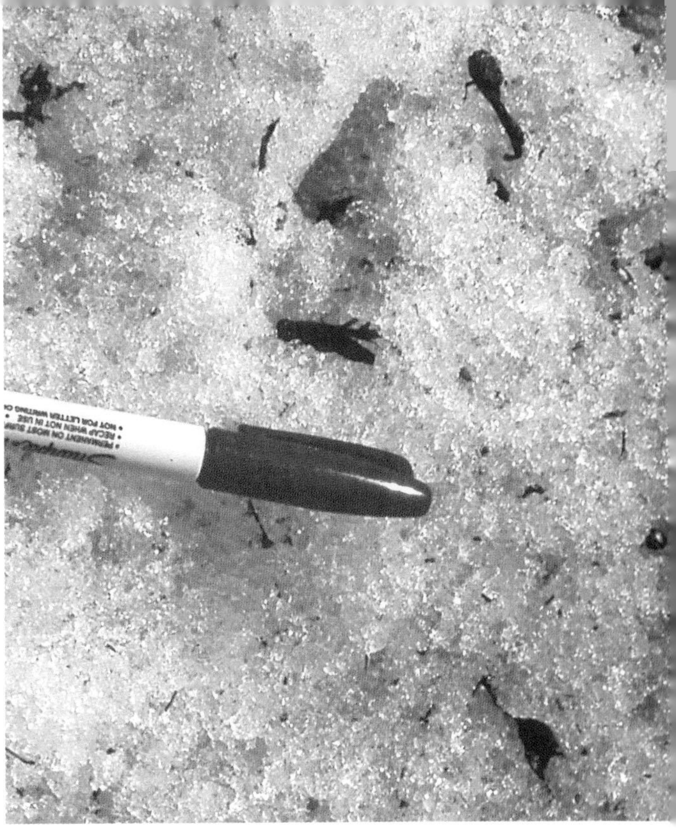

Lockwood turned up a specimen. Smaller than a pen cap, this locust from the past can teach us about today's locusts.

Then Lockwood learned that Rocky Mountain locusts all gathered in the river valleys of the Rocky Mountains to lay their eggs. During the 1800s, the gold and silver industries boomed in these same river valleys. The nesting area of the Rocky Mountain locust became bustling and overcrowded.

"The killer of the Rocky Mountain locust turns out to be us," said Lockwood. As farmers flocked to the river valleys to feed the miners, they plowed up the fields. The plowing destroyed the delicate eggs that had been laid by the great swarm. Because the eggs did not mature into full-grown locusts, the species was entirely destroyed. The only extinction of a pest species in agricultural history was an accident! The lesson gained on locust extermination could help modern people in countries where locust swarms are still doing damage.

Like locusts, some swarming animals fly. Some march, some crawl, and some swim. They may swarm for food, for breeding, or for new homes. Swarms may harm humans, benefit humans, or not affect humans at all, but they all help the swarming species survive.

Check In How were the Rocky Mountain locusts killed off?

Discuss

1. Tell about some of the ways you think the four pieces in this book are linked.
2. What are some different ways swarming benefits animals?
3. Compare and contrast the life cycle of a cicada with the life cycle of an army ant.
4. What is it that causes locusts to swarm? What effect can this swarming have on humans?
5. What questions do you still have about animal swarms? What can you do to find out more?